DATE DUE		
JAN 12 '01		
MAY 4 '01		
FEB 5 '02		
APR 19 '02		
MAR 23 '06		

9 / 00

JACKSON
COUNTY
Library Services

HEADQUARTERS
413 West Main Street
Medford, Oregon 97501

SHELLS

SHELLS

CHARTWELL
BOOKS, INC.

Published by Chartwell Books
A Division of Book Sales Inc.
114 Northfield Avenue
Edison, New Jersey 08837
USA

ISBN 0-7858-0973-2

This book is produced by
Quantum Books Ltd
6 Blundell Street
London N7 9BH

Project Manager: Rebecca Kingsley
Project Editor: Judith Millidge
Design/Editorial: David Manson
Andy McColm, Maggie Manson

The material in this publication previously appeared in
Rocks, Shells, Fossils, Minerals and Gems,
Encyclopedia of Shells

QUMSPSL
Set in Futura
Reproduced in Singapore by Eray Scan
Printed in Singapore by Star Standard Industries (Pte) Ltd

Contents

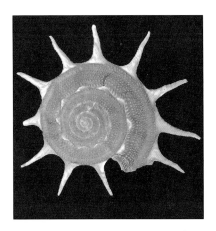

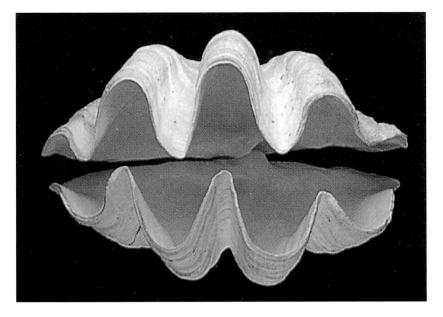

SENSATIONAL SHELLS

Scientifically known as marine molluscs, seashells are the hard outer covering of highly adaptable snails that inhabit the world's oceans in a wide range of environments and at varying depths. These shells are found washed ashore, emptied of the soft bodies that once inhabited them. The appreciation and enjoyment of their beauty is probably as widespread now as at any time in history.

The Influence of Shells

The shell has been inextricably linked with the human story since the dawn of civilization. There are many examples of man's widespread use of shells for decorative and practical purposes throughout history.

SHELLS AS FOOD

Discarded shells have been found in the waste-heaps of prehistoric settlements, but the Romans may have been the first people to farm molluscs, particularly oysters, as a food source. Today, nearly every nation with a seashore has its own speciality. In the Philippines, people in some areas consume every mollusc fished, even the toxic cone shells, which are boiled and eaten with rice. The USA is famous for her abalone steaks and clam chowder, while French cuisine boasts the culinary delights of *coquilles St Jacques* and *moules marinieres*.

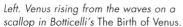

Left. Venus rising from the waves on a scallop in Botticelli's The Birth of Venus.

Above. Thatcheria mirabilis, *inspired Frank Lloyd Wright's architectural designs.*

SHELLS AS CURRENCY

In times past, the use of cowrie shells as a form of currency was widespread in Asia, Central Africa, the Indian Ocean and the Malaysian islands. Easy to collect and handle they were strung into lengths for bartering. The North American Indians used to grind down pieces of bivalves and use them for trading. Certain clams were pierced and strung on sinew, the most prized shells being those with a purple interior.

SHELLS IN ART

Of all shells, the scallop has been perhaps the greatest source of inspiration for artists. Chosen by Botticelli as a vehicle for Venus rising from the waves, and in modern times picked as the logo for the Shell Oil Company. Leonardo made drawings of spiral shells as a basis for spiral staircases and the Guggenheim Museum in New York designed by Frank Lloyd Wright is said to be inspired by *Thatcheria mirabilis.*

Fossil Shells

With the wealth and complexity of natural molluscan design, it is hard to believe that they all simply "just happened". Science argues that molluscs derive from a unifying original life form, but the evolution of molluscs cannot easily be traced.

THE LINK WITH THE PAST

Some genera clearly developed and changed under environmental influences, while others ceased to exist, but there is no scientifically proven common ancestor of all mollusc species known today. Several present-day species, such as chambered nautilus shells, have unsevered links with very early geological times. These incredible shells have withstood the passage of time without noticeable change while other less sophisticated and adaptable species, have totally disappeared and are known only as fossils. There is a vast range of molluscs, often with bizarre shapes, which can only be found in fossil form. These very early species provide a fascinating subject for study.

GEOLOGICAL KEY

ERA	PERIOD	MILLIONS OF YEARS
TERTIARY	Pliocene	5–10
	Eocene	40–70
MESOZOIC	Jurassic	200
PALAEOZOIC	Carboniferous	350
	Devonian	400
	Cambrian	500–600

Geological periods referred to in text; dating according to scientific estimate.

Above. A halved and polished section of a Jurassic ammonite. Note its similarity to the Nautilus shells of today (see p.62).

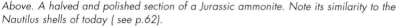

Gastropods, bivalves, scaphopods and bivalves are all well represented in fossil records, however, species of the order Polyplacophora, although first appearing in the late Cambrian period, are scarce and rare. Monoplacophora, another very ancient group, also date back to early Cambrian. With the onset of the Mesozoic era, a great increase in generic variation took place, especially among shells of the Volutidae, Muricidae and Cerithiidae families.

During the Tertiary era, the Eocene period especially, the Gastropods were the most numerous of all molluscs, and many species have changed very little from that time to the present day.

Significant numbers of bivalves did not appear until the late Devonian and early Carboniferous periods when the swampy conditions appear to have suited them better than previous conditions and they began to thrive.

Shell Habitat

Seashells are able to inhabit almost any environment where water can offer an adequate supply of food. The majority of species, however, and certainly the most highly colored and patterned shells, exist in shallow waters.

SEA AND SEASHORE

Intertidal. The area between the highest and lowest tides.

Sub-tidal. The shallow water zone, including waters below the low tide line and coral reefs.

Abyssal. The deep-water zone, the dark regions down to the ocean floor.

MUDDY HABITATS

Many species thrive in sand or in muddy habitats, and burrowing shells such as olives, mitres and numerous bivalves, find sandy substrates ideal. Mangrove swamps also provide a food-rich habitat for numerous species such as horn shells and mud creepers.

Above. Calliostoma zizyphinum, lives in the shallow waters of western Europe.

Left. Numerous varieties of shells can be collected on the beach at low tide.

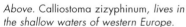

ROCKY COASTS

On rocky coasts, where tougher condition prevail, you will find species with strongly constructed shells, such as limpets, top shells and chitons, that are adapted to cling to rock faces and boulders without being washed away. Other less sturdy species tend to live under rocks and slabs or in rocky crevices.

CORAL REEFS

Coral reefs are an ideal habitat for numerous species of mollusc, and here the majority of the highly colored and attractive shells are found, mostly in tropical waters.

DEEP WATER DWELLERS

So-called pelagic species live on or near the surface of the sea away from shores and land attached to a 'raft' of bubbles. In deep water or abyssal zones other well-adapted species exist. They are often thin walled whitish or mostly colorless shells.

The Phylum Mollusca

All living things are grouped by classification into major sections known as phyla. The phylum Mollusca is second in numerical size to the Arthropoda (insects) with more than 100,00 species. It is divided into six smaller sections which are referred to as classes.

CLASS GASTROPODA

At least three-quarters of the world's molluscs are gastropods and nearly half the species are marine including limpets, cowries, murex, cones and olives.

CLASS BIVALVIA

The outer shell of a bivalve comprises two pieces, or valves, hinged by a ligament. Includes oysters, mussels, cockles, clams.

CLASS CEPHALOPODA

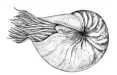

Highly mobile with large eyes, tentacles and powerful mouths. Some have shells, such as the Nautilus, while others such as the squid and the octopus have none.

CLASS SCAPHOPODA

Known as tusk or tooth shells these are the most primitive of all the molluscs. They have no head, eyes or gills, but possess a large foot and a radula.

CLASS POLYPLACOPHORA

Known as chitons, they resemble woodlice, and have eight segmented plates held together together by a leathery girdle.

CLASS MONOPLACOPHORA

The earliest known gastropods were thought until this century to be extinct. They are exceptionally rare and are seldom if ever found in amateur collections.

How to Use this Book

The information in the directory is arranged to supply the reader with a snapshot of information about each species. A number of key icons are used throughout the book to reinforce the information visually. These are explained below.

SENSATIONAL SHELLS

SHAPE AND SIZE
Stylized shape with size given in inches.

Gastropods:
Cones, murex, volutes

Gastropods:
Limpets, cowries, olives

Bivalves:
Scallops, clams, cockles

Cephalopods:
Nautilus, paper nautilus

HABITAT DEPTH
All figures are approximate and some species may be found at more than one depth.

Extends to 83ft

Between 83 and 495ft

Between 495 and 1,650ft

ABUNDANCE

Rare

 Uncommon

Common Abundant

THROUGHOUT THE DIRECTORY

The scientific name for each species is given first in bold capitals followed by the common name in smaller roman capitals, for example:

PATELLA GRANATINA
SANDPAPER LIMPET

SHELL SPECIES

Conchology— the study and collecting of shells—is a broad enough subject to encompass people of all ages and at every level of commitment, from the amateur to the scientist. Some people collect shells simply because they appreciate such natural objects, others because they derive artistic pleasure from their varied shapes and colors, while for others shell collecting has become an obsession.

HALIOTUS ASININA ASS'S EAR ABALONE

This curved smooth shell is elongated in shape and is aptly named. The exterior is a pale olive green, enlivened with odd splashes of brown. The interior is white with hints of green. For the size of the shell, the holes are very large.

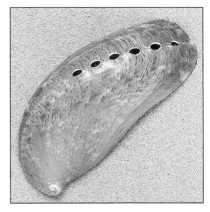

Family Haliotidae (Abalones).
Class Gastropoda.
Super family Pleurotomarioidea.
Size 8in.
Locality Central Indo-Pacific.
Habitat depth To 83ft.

8in

FISSURELLA PERUVIANA PERUVIAN KEYHOLE LIMPET

A small rounded shell with a pointed conical spire, it has relatively straight sides and is pale crimson in color, with wide dark greyish-brown rays.
The small hole is edged in cream. The interior is white with a crimson margin.

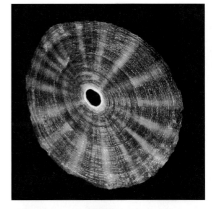

Family Fissurellidae (Keyhole Limpets).
Class Gastropoda.
Super family Fissurelloidea.
Size 2.5cm (1in).
Locality Western South America.
Habitat depth To 25m (83ft).

1in
(2.5cm)

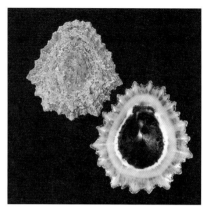

PATELLA GRANATINA SANDPAPER LIMPET

This has a rather stout shell, with sharply angular radial ridges. On mature specimens the dorsum is usually partly eroded away due to the conditions of its habitat. The color ranges from gray to beige. Interior colors vary, although there is always a large dark brown central scar.

Family Pattellidae (True Limpets).
Class Gastropoda.
Super family Patelloidea.
Size 3¹/₄ in.
Locality South Africa.
Habitat depth To 83ft.

PATELLA GRANULARIS GRANULAR LIMPET

The shell is smallish with radiating ribs. Large shells can be eroded on the spire. The interior bears a large brown central scar on a background that is usually a pale blue-gray. There is a thick dark grey or black marginal rim, indented with shallow grooves.

Family Pattellidae (True Limpets).
Class Gastropoda.
Super family Patelloidea.
Size 2¹/₂ in.
Locality South Africa.
Habitat depth To 83ft.

CALLIOSTOMA MONILE MONILE TOP

This is a pretty and delicate little shell with straight sides and a tall spire. There are minute spiral striae on the whorls. The color is pale beige with a dominant band running above the sutures of pale purple squares and 'flames' on white. It lives on sponges in shallow water.

Family Trochidae (Top Shells).
Class Gastropoda.
Super family Trochoidea.
Size ³/₄ in.
Locality Western Australia.
Habitat depth To 83ft.

  ³/₄in

MAUREA PUNCTULATA PUNCTATE MAUREA

A short rather squat species, with a large rounded body whorl, it bears many rows of fine spiral cording. The background color is beige or mid-brown and the cords bear alternate white and brown dots and dashes. These specimens were found on rocks at low tide, Mahanga Beach, New Zealand.

Family Trochidae (Top Shells).
Class Gastropoda.
Super family Trochoidea.
Size 1¹/₂ in.
Locality New Zealand.
Habitat depth To 83ft.

 1¹/₂in

ANGARIA TYRIA TYRIA DELPHINULA

Two forms of this extremely variable
species are depicted here. Some
experts would put *A.tyria* as yet
a further form of *A. delphinulus*. The
smaller of the two is probably a
Philippine shell, whereas the larger
was fished off North-West Australia.
Extremely variable.

Family Turbinidae (Turban Shells).
Class Gastropoda.
Super family Trochoidea.
Size 2³/₄ in.
Locality South-West Pacific and
Australia.
Habitat depth 83–495ft.

NINELLA WHITLEYI WHITLEY'S TURBAN

When well-cleaned, *N.whitleyi* is an
attractive shell with a strongly ridged
shoulder bearing bumps and low
nodules. The shell is overlaid with a
pattern of sharp diagonal ridges and
is a beige grey, some specimens
bearing pale green streaks. The spire
is flat and often eroded.

Family Turbinidae (Turban Shells).
Class Gastropoda.
Super family Trochoidea.
Size 2¹/₄ in.
Locality Australia.
Habitat depth To 83ft.

GUILDFORDIA TRIUMPHANS TRIUMPHANT STAR

Another almost flat shell with a low spire, this has long projecting spines at right angles to the body whorl and much fine spiral beading overall. The color is pink-toned bronze and the base is off-white to cream. The operculum is white and ovate. A collector's favorite. It is a deep-water species.

Family Turbinidae (Turban Shells).
Class Gastropoda.
Super family Trochoidea.
Size 2¹/₄ in.
Locality Taiwan and Japan.
Habitat depth 495–1650ft.

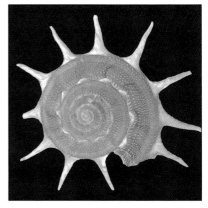

PHASIANELLA VENTRICOSA SWOLLEN PHEASANT

Although in texture it is identical to *P. australis,* the shape of *P. ventricosa* differs in that the spire is relatively low and the body whorl large and bulbous. Patterns and colors can be extremely variable. The operculum is white and calcareous.

Family Phasianellidae (Pheasant Shells).
Class Gastropoda.
Super family Trochoidea.
Size 2¹/₄ in.
Locality Southern Australia.
Habitat depth To 83ft.

CLYPEOLUM LATISSIMUM WIDE NERITE

A species with an unusual shape, this is one of several in the subgenus *Clypeolum*. It has a wide flaring mouth and a broad parietal shield. The exterior coloring is brown, gray or pale mauve, decorated with a fine black netted pattern.

Family Neritidae (Nerites).
Class Gastropoda.
Super family Neritoidea.
Size 1¼ in.
Locality Western Central America.
Habitat depth To 83ft.

1¼in ★
      ★ ★

CERITHIUM MUSCARUM FLY-SPECKED CERITH

A small slender species, with coarse spiral nodules, it is middle-to-dark brown. The nodules, which in some shells are joined axially into ridges, are off white. This is a shallow-water species— the two depicted were collected from Tarpoon Beach, Florida.

Family Cerithiidae (Cerith Shells).
Class Gastropoda.
Super family Cerithioidea.
Size 1in.
Locality Southern Florida, West Indies.
Habitat depth To 83ft.

1in ★ ★
     ★ ★

TURRITELLA CINGULATA BANDED SCREW SHELL

A short solid species, it is cream in color, with several rows of broad dark brown spiral bands. The whorls are generally straight sided and number between eight and ten. It lives in subtidal waters. The shell depicted here was fished at Tongoy, Chile.

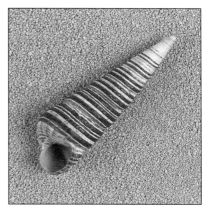

Family Turritellidae (Screw Shells).
Class Gastropoda.
Super family Cerithioidea.
Size 3in.
Locality Chile.
Habitat depth To 83ft.

  3in

TURRITELLA GONOSTOMA ANGLE-MOUTHED SCREW SHELL

Similar in shape to *T. broderipiana*, it is slightly smaller, and perhaps the suture is more impressed and the pattern— a cream background with large axial patches and streaks of dark gray or black—is more evident. There are very fine spiral striae.

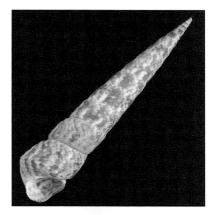

Family Turritellidae (Screw Shells).
Class Gastropoda.
Super family Cerithioidea.
Size 4¹/₄ in.
Locality Western Central America.
Habitat depth To 83ft.

  4¹/₄in

APORRHAIS SERRESIANUS MEDITERRANEAN PELICAN'S FOOT

Although similar to *A. pesgaline*, this is smaller, usually white or off-white and has four projections, two of which are partly joined, and a siphonal canal. There are three spiral rows of nodulose ribbing on the body whorl and one row thereafter to the apex.

Family Aporrhaidae (Pelican's Foot Shells).
Class Gastropoda.
Super family Stromboidea.
Size 1³/₄ in.
Locality Mediterranean.
Habitat depth 495–1650ft.

1³/₄in

LAMBIS LAMBIS COMMON SPIDER CONCH

One of the most well-known of shells, this differs from *L. truncata* in that it is much smaller and has large rounded nodules on the body whorl. Of the two depicted specimens, the deep orange form is a rarer, larger variation from Western Australia. The female is generally larger and has longer projections.

Family Strombidae (Conch Shells).
Class Gastropoda.
Super family Strombidae.
Size 8in.
Locality Indo-Pacific.
Habitat depth To 83ft.

To 8in

STROMBUS TRICORNIS THREE-KNOBBED CONCH

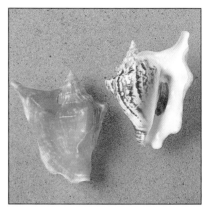

Although there are many rounded nodules on the shoulders, there are usually two or three that are larger, and it is from these that the common name is derived. A smaller conch, it has a wide lip that extends into a finger-like projection at the posterior. Colors and patterns vary greatly. It is found in shallow water on sand and is endemic.

Family Strombidae (Conch Shells).
Class Gastropoda.
Super family Stromboidea.
Size 4in.
Locality Red Sea, Gulf of Aden.
Habitat depth To 83ft.

  4in

STROMBUS GALLUS ROOSTER TAIL CONCH

A distinctive shell, it has a very pronounced process which extends upward from the posterior lip margin, suggesting a rooster's tail. The relatively low spire is nodulose and the shoulder of the body whorl bears four or five strong high rounded nodules. The lip margin is slightly undulating.

Family Strombidae (Conch Shells).
Class Gastropoda.
Super family Stromboidea.
Size 4³/4 in.
Locality Caribbean to Brazil.
Habitat depth To 83ft.

 4³/4 in

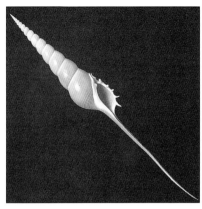

TIBIA FUSUS SPINDLE TIBIA

This shell has a very tall slender spire of about 19 whorls and a long narrow canal. There are five finger-like projections on the lip margin and the anal canal is curved against the side of the body whorl. There are fine axial ridges on the early whorls. The aperture and columella are white.

Family Strombidae (Conch Shells).
Class Gastropoda.
Super family Stromboidea.
Size 9in.
Locality Philippines.
Habitat depth 83–495ft.

  9in ★ ★ ★

TIBIA MARTINI MARTIN'S TIBIA

This generally thin and lightweight shell has rounded whorls and a fairly short straight siphonal canal. There are four or five very stunted denticles on the lip margin. A one-time rarity, it has now become readily available, due to deep-sea commercial fishing in the late 1960s.

Family Strombidae (Conch Shells).
Class Gastropoda.
Super family Stromboidea.
Size 4³/₄ in.
Locality Philippines.
Habitat depth 495–1650ft.

  4³/₄in ★ ★ ★

CYPRAEA CINEREA ATLANTIC GRAY COWRIE

A sturdy little shell, with a rather humped dorsum and convex base, it has fine grooved teeth at either side of a curved aperture. The color is a pinky gray, overlaid with black dots and blotches, more so at the margins, which are slightly inflated on mature specimens.

Family Cypraeidae (Cowrie Shells).
Class Gastropoda.
Super family Cypraeidae.
Size 1¹⁄₄ in.
Locality South-Eastern USA to Brazil.
Habitat depth To 83ft.

  1¼in

CYPRAEA AURANTIUM GOLDEN COWRIE

Highly prized among collectors, the purchase price is usually totally out of proportion to its rarity. Demand exceeds supply. The large ovate and inflated shell is not 'golden' in fact, but a deep magenta when fresh, fading to a deep orange. The base is pinkish beige and the teeth are tinged with orange.

Family Cypraeidae (Cowrie Shells).
Class Gastropoda.
Super family Cypraeoidae.
Size 4in.
Locality Philippines, Solomon Islands and Fiji.
Habitat depth 83–495ft.

 4in

CYPRAEA TEULEREI TEULERE'S COWRIE

Once a great rarity, this endemic shell eventually came to be collected in great numbers in the late 1960s, after its habitat had been discovered. A thick and heavy, irregularly-shaped species, it has distinctive markings and no teeth.

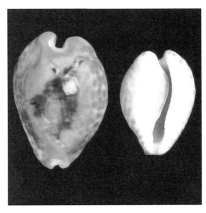

Family Strombidae (Conch Shells).
Class Gastropoda.
Super family Cypraeoidae.
Size 2in.
Locality Gulf of Oman (Masirah Island).
Habitat depth To 83ft.

CYPRAEA ROSSELLI ROSSELL'S COWRIE

Probably the rarest of the sub-genus Zoila, and almost deltoid in shape, with a steeply humped dorsum. It is a very rich dark brown to black, usually with a creamy white and irregularly patched dorsum. A moderately deep-water species, it is collected in crayfish pots or by scuba divers.

Family Cypraeidae (Cowrie Shells).
Class Gastropoda.
Super family Cypraeidae.
Size 2in.
Locality Western South America.
Habitat depth 83–495ft.

CYPHOMA GIBBOSUM FLAMINGO TONGUE

A thick solid calloused shell, with a strong rounded spiral ridge. It has no teeth on its lip. In color, it is creamy apricot, with a slender area of white along the dorsum. The base and aperture are creamy white.

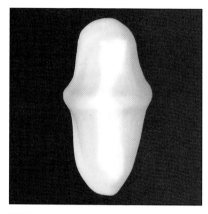

Family Ovulidae (Egg Shells).
Class Gastropoda.
Super family Cypraeoidea.
Size 1¹/₄ in.
Locality South-Eastern USA to Brazil.
Habitat depth To 83ft.

NATICA JANTHOSTOMOIDES

This endemic very rounded moon shell has a silky lustre and fine axial growth lines. The exterior color is beige, with spiral bands and axial lines of pale brown. The calcareous operculum is off-white and is grooved.

Family Naticidae (Moon or Necklace Shells).
Class Gastropoda.
Super family Naticoidea.
Size 1¹/₄ in.
Locality Japan.
Habitat depth 283–495ft.

NATICA TURTONI TURTON'S MOON

Another of the scarce West African species, this has similar markings to those of *N. alapapilionis,* but differs slightly in that the spire is somewhat sloping and the shell is almost twice the size. The pattern is quite similar.

Family Naticidae (Moon or Necklace Shells).
Class Gastropoda.
Super family Naticoidea.
Size 1³/₄ in.
Locality Western South America.
Habitat depth 83–495ft.

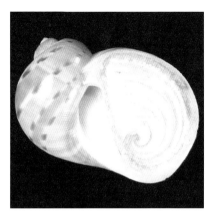

  1³/₄in

TANEA ZELANDICA NEW ZEALAND MOON

A very rounded shell, with a low spire and enlarged body whorl, it is beige or light brown, with spiral bands of broken pale to mid-brown squares or irregular shapes. The aperture and surrounding area is white. The umbilicus is closed by a large funicle.

Family Naticidae (Moon or Necklace Shells).
Class Gastropoda.
Super family Naticoidea.
Size 1¹/₄ in.
Locality New Zealand.
Habitat depth To 83ft.

 1¹/₄in

TONNA SULCOSA BANDED TUN

A medium-sized species, it has a
moderate spire. The body whorl is
ovate and bears rather flattened spiral
cords. The periphery of the aperture is
stepped and the lower edge dentate.
The siphonal canal is deep and
pronounced.

Family Tonnidae (Tun Shells).
Class Gastropoda.
Super family Tonoidea.
Size 4in.
Locality Indo-Pacific.
Habitat depth 83–495ft.

 To 4in

TONNA DOLIUM SPOTTED TUN

A well-known species, incorrectly
referred to as *T.tessellata*, it is much
larger than the latter and lacks lip
denticles. The whorls bear low rounded
cords, with brown squares or regular
blotches. The columella is 'twisted'.
There is a rich brown tinting inside
the aperture.

Family Tonnidae (Tun Shells).
Class Gastropoda.
Super family Tonoidea.
Size 4³⁄₄ in.
Locality Western Pacific, New Zealand.
Habitat depth 83–495ft.

 4¾in

T O N N I D A E

TONNA LUTEOSTOMA   GOLD-MOUTHED TUN

A rounded heavy species, with a low spire and moderately channelled suture, it has prominent rounded spiral cords. The columella is glazed and covers part of the small umbilicus. The outer shell is creamy white, with orange brown streaks and blotches.

Family Tonnidae (Tun Shells).
Class Gastropoda.
Super family Tonoidea.
Size 4³/₄ in.
Locality Western Pacific.
Habitat depth 83–495ft.

XENOPHALIUM PYRUM PYRUM   PEAR BONNET

A fairly solid globose shell, with a low spire, it is usually bears weak nodules on the shoulder of the whorl. The lip is smooth, as is the undulating columella. The background color is pale beige gray, with pale brown spiral streaks.

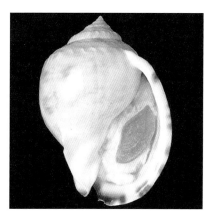

Family Cassidae (Helmet or Bonnet Shells).
Class Gastropoda.
Super family Tonoidea.
Size 3in.
Locality Southern Australia, New Zealand.
Habitat depth Between 495–1650ft.

T O N N I D A E / C A S S I D A E

SEMICASSIS GRANULATUM GRANULATUM SCOTCH BONNET

A stocky ovate shell, with a medium spire, the Scotch Bonnet has fine spiral grooves and faint axial growth striae. The lip is thickened, recurved and dentate, and there are pustules on the columella and on the shield.

Family Cassidae (Helmet or Bonnet Shells).
Class Gastropoda.
Super family Tonoidea.
Size 3in.
Locality South-Eastern USA to Brazil.
Habitat depth 83–495ft.

  3in

BIPLEX PERCA WINGED OR MAPLE LEAF TRITON

Huge specimens of this deep water shell used to be fished regularly off Taiwan. Shells half the size now come from the Philippines. The winged triton has an amazing shape—very flat with wide leaf-like axially aligned varices.

Family Ranellidae (The Tritons).
Class Gastropoda.
Super family Tonoidea.
Size 2³/4 in.
Locality Western Pacific.
Habitat depth 495–1650ft.

  2¾in

CABESTANA CUTACEA MEDITERRANEAN BARK TRITON

A shell with angular whorls, the color is pale brown throughout, and the lip is heavily dentate. The shell dwells in moderately deep water, this specimen coming from Southern Italy.

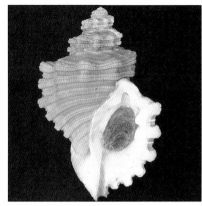

Family Ranellidae (The Tritons).
Class Gastropoda.
Super family Tonoidea.
Size 3in.
Locality North-east Atlantic, Mediterranean.
Habitat depth 495–1650ft.

3in

CYMATIUM PERRYI PERRY'S TRITON

Solid and heavy, with a medium spire, this species is dominated by angular knobbed whorls and rounded ribbed varices. Its colors are striking—pale orange or tan, with cream and dark brown ribs. The dentate inner lip and columella are a reddish orange. The small operculum is ovate and horny. The canal is long and curved.

Family Ranellidae (The Tritons).
Class Gastropoda.
Super family Tonoidea.
Size 4in.
Locality Southern India, Sri Lanka.
Habitat depth 83–495ft.

4in

R
A
N
E
L
L
I
D
A
E

CYMATIUM AQUITILE AQUATILE HAIRY TRITON

A tall elongate-fusiform species, which is thick and heavy. The orange tan whorls bear low cords and fine spiral grooves, and there are low rounded knobbed ribs. The inner lip carries a double row of strong denticles and the columella and parietal area have many folds.

Family Ranellidae (The Tritons).
Class Gastropoda.
Super family Tonoidea.
Size 2^1/$_2$ in.
Locality Indo-Pacific.
Habitat depth To 83ft.

  2½in

CHARONIA TRITONIS TRUMPET TRITON

The largest species in the triton family, this is a well-known and very beautiful shell, with a tall spire, rounded whorls, and a large flaring lip. The markings are distinctive and the deep orange aperture is particularly attractive. This is one of several shells used as a form of trumpet once the apex has been removed, and a very popular collectors' shell.

Family Ranellidae (The Tritons).
Class Gastropoda.
Super family Tonoidea.
Size 16in.
Locality Indo-Pacific.
Habitat depth To 83ft.

 16in

CYMATIUM PFEIFFERIANUM PFEIFFER'S HAIRY TRITON

An elongate-fusiform shape, it has a tall spire and a long canal. Numerous beaded cords and axial riblets ornament the whorls, giving a cancelled effect. It is variable in color, and the two forms shown here were collected off Phuket, Thailand, in shallow water.

Family Ranellidae (The Tritons).
Class Gastropoda.
Super family Tonoidea.
Size 3in.
Locality Indo-Pacific.
Habitat depth To 83ft.

  To 3in

SASSIA SUBDISTORTA DISTORTED ROCK TRITON

The distorted rock triton has a tall spire, rather angular whorls and a short siphonal canal. There are spirally beaded cords, most prominent at the middle to upper part of the whorl. Two color forms are shown here.

Family Ranellidae (The Tritons).
Class Gastropoda.
Super family Tonoidea.
Size 2in.
Locality Southern Australia, Tasmania.
Habitat depth To 83ft.

  2in

BUFONARIA ELEGANS ELEGANT FROG

An attractive and rather lightweight shell, it features spiral beading, axially aligned varices and low sharp nodules on the whorls. The varices support larger sharper nodules—virtually spines in many cases. The color is cream or pale brown, with narrow spiral bands of dark brown.

Family Bursidae (Frog Shells).
Class Gastropoda.
Super family Tonoidea.
Size 3in.
Locality Indian Ocean.
Habitat depth To 83ft.

 3in ★ / ★ ★

BUFONARIA NOBILIS NOBLE FROG

Another laterally 'flattened' species, with axially aligned varices, it has a tall spire and a large aperture with an expanded lip. There are numerous spiral rows of beading and low nodules both on the whorls and varices.

Family Bursidae (Frog Shells).
Class Gastropoda.
Super family Tonoidea.
Size 3¹/₂ in.
Locality Western Pacific.
Habitat depth To 495ft.

  3½in ★ / ★ ★

B U R S I D A E

EPITONIUM SCALARE PRECIOUS WENTLETRAP

A world-famous shell and once a great rarity, it is now available in appreciable numbers, coming mainly from Taiwan and the Philippines. It is spectacular, comprising loose rounded whorls separated by strong blade-like varices, which are connected to each other at the open suture line.

Family Epitoniidae (Wentletraps).
Class Gastropoda.
Super family Epitonioidea.
Size 2¹/₄ in.
Locality Japan to Northern Australia.
Habitat depth To 83ft.

   To 2¼in

STHENORYTIS PERNOBILIS NOBLE WENKLETRAP

An extremely rare and sought-after species, it is only very occasionally live-taken—usually in fish or lobster traps—and is reputed to live as deep as 4950ft. This specimen was inhabited by a hermit crab and collected at 594ft in Barbados.

Family Epitoniidae (Wentletraps).
Class Gastropoda.
Super family Epitonioidea.
Size 1 in.
Locality Caribbean.
Habitat depth 495–1650ft.

   1in

CHICOREUS NOBILIS NOBLE MUREX

A small, very beautiful shell of a deep pink color, with fine spiral threads of mid-brown. There are three varices per whorl, and each bears medium-length frondose spines decreasing in size towards the posterior; the canal is long, slightly recurved and also spinose.

Family Muricidae (Rock Shells.
Class Gastropoda.
Super family Muricoidea.
Size 2in.
Locality Japan to Philippines.
Habitat depth To 495ft.

CHICOREUS PALMAROSAE ROSE-BRANCHED MUREX

The Rose-Branched Murex is superbly beautiful and aptly named—the lovely pink fronds do resemble rose branches. Shells are difficult to clean, heavily encrusted with marine debris and lime, but the care and time spent cleaning is well rewarded.

Family Muricidae (Rock Shells).
Class Gastropoda.
Super family Muricoidea.
Size 4in.
Locality Sri Lanka.
Habitat depth To 83ft.

MUREX PECTEN VENUS COMB MUREX

The most spinose member of the *Murex* genus, this shell is adorned with long, closed spines. The whorls are rounded and bulbous, bearing numerous spiral cords. The inner lip is expanded and raised adjacent to the columella.

Family Muricidae (Rock Shells).
Class Gastropoda.
Super family Muricoidea.
Size 6in.
Locality Indo-Pacific.
Habitat depth To 83ft.

PTERYNOTUS MIYOKOAE MIYOKO MUREX

A very beautiful species, the Miyoko murex features dominant wing-like varices which are finely ridged and lamellate. A fine collectors' item, endemic to the Philippines, perfect examples are keenly sought-after.

Family Muricidae (Rock Shells).
Class Gastropoda.
Super family Muricoidea.
Size 2¹/₄ in.
Locality Cebu, Philippines.
Habitat depth 495–1650ft.

PTERYNOTUS LOEBBECKEI LOEBBECKE'S MUREX

Closely resembling *P. miyokoae,* this tends to be rather heavier, and more stoutly built. The color is usually a plain pale orange with no spiral bands. A great rarity for many years, this beautiful species remains a choice collectors' item, and perfect shells still command high prices.

Family Muricidae (Rock Shells).
Class Gastropoda.
Super family Muricoidea.
Size 2¹/₂in.
Locality Southern Japan to Philippines.
Habitat depth 495–1650ft.

2½in

MUREXIELLA BOJADORENSIS

A sought-after collectors' item from off-shore waters, this has a low spire, long straight canal, and four or five strong varices. The coarse spines are scaly and those at the shoulders are thickest and longest, the extremities being foliated and recurved. Specimens can be off-white, cream, or mid-to-dark brown.

Family Muricidae (Rock Shells).
Class Gastropoda.
Super family Muricoidea.
Size 1³/₄in.
Locality Western South America.
Habitat depth To 495ft.

1¾in

MURICIDAE

NUCELLA LAPILLUS ATLANTIC DOG WHELK

This sturdy little shell lives on rocks and feeds on mussels and other molluscs. It is ovate, with a low narrow spire and enlarged body whorl bearing rounded spiral cords. It is very variable in color and banding, several forms being shown here, all of them coming from Cornwall, England.

Family Muricidae (Rock Shells).
Class Gastropoda.
Super family Muricoidea.
Size 1 1/2in.
Locality North-West and North-East Atlantic coasts.
Habitat depth To 83ft.

BABELOMUREX JAPONICUS JAPANESE LATIAXIS

Two specimens are shown of this lovely shell, both fished in deep water off Taiwan. The outstanding features are spinose ridges and small triangular spines, occasionally recurved, at the shoulders. Shells are generally off-white with a pure white aperture.

Family Muricidae (Rock Shells).
Class Gastropoda.
Super family Muricoidea.
Size 1 1/2in.
Locality Japan to Philippines.
Habitat depth 495–1650ft.

MURICIDAE

LATIAXIA MAWAE MAWE'S LATIAXIS

A strangely shaped and very popular latiaxis, its spire is flat or depressed, and the convex sides of the whorls taper at the anterior. The body whorl uncoils, developing to a very broad expanded area that includes the gaping umbilicus and open recurved canal.

Family Coralliophilidae (Latiaxis Shells).
Class Gastropoda.
Super family Muricoidea.
Size 2in.
Locality Japan, Taiwan, Philippines.
Habitat depth To 495ft.

  2in

BABYLONIA AMBULACRUM WALKWAY BABYLON

Rather similar to *B. spirata*, the Walkway Babylon is smaller and more bulbous, the suture channels are narrower; the general color tends to be an olive brown; and the pattern is closer and resembles a snakeskin. The umbilicus is wide and deep.

Family Buccinidae (Whelks).
Class Gastropoda.
Super family Muricoidea.
Size 1¹/₂ in.
Locality Western Pacific.
Habitat depth To 495ft.

  1½in

CANTHARUS MELANOSTOMUS BLACK-MOUTHED GOBLET WHELK

A smallish ovate and coarsely sculptured shell, it has numerous spiral cords and very low broad axial ribs, strongest at the shoulders. It is a rich tan with a distinctive brown or black columella and parietal wall. The lip is dentate and there are moderate lirae within.

Family Buccinidae (Whelks).
Class Gastropoda.
Super family Muricoidea.
Size 2in.
Locality Indian Ocean, Philippines.
Habitat depth To 83ft.

  2 in

BUSYCON CANALICULATUM CHANNELLED WHELK

The channelled whelk has a low spire, and straight-sided whorls, angled at the shoulders into a deeply channelled suture. The enlarged body whorl tapers into a long open siphonal canal. The depicted specimen, which is from Florida, has axial patterning.

Family Melongenidae (Crown Conch, Swamp Conch).
Class Gastropoda.
Super family Muricoidea.
Size 6in.
Locality Cape Cod to Florida.
Habitat depth To 83ft.

 6in

MELONGENA CORONA FLORIDA CROWN CONCH

A large attractive shell, the Florida crown conch has distinctive coronated shoulders. There are very fine axial striae and coarse strong growth lines. The color varies; a few are creamy white throughout, most are banded spirally with brown, gray and pale orange.

Family Melongenidae (Crown Conch, Swamp Conch).
Class Gastropoda.
Super family Muricoidea.
Size 4in.
Locality Florida to North-Eastern Mexico.
Habitat depth To 83ft.

   4in ★ ★★

PLEUROPLOCA TRAPEZIUM FOX HEAD

A large, thick and heavy shell, fusiform in shape with angular whorls. The lip is dentate, and there are numerous fine raised lirae within. The columella is smooth. The shells are either an all-over beige or light brown, or have orange tints and almost-black spiral lines.

Family Fasciolariidae (Tulip and Spindle Shells),
Class Gastropoda.
Super family Muricoidea.
Size 7½ in.
Locality Indo-Pacific.
Habitat depth To 83ft.

  7½in ★ ★★

LATIRUS POLYGONUS POLYGON LATIRUS

A solidly built shell, with a spire of
medium height and a fairly short open
canal, it has strong rounded axial ribs
and nodules that are usually low but
sharp, and most prominent at the
shoulders. Attractively colored with dark
brown spiral bands on a white or pale
orange background.

Family Fasciolariidae (Tulip and
Spindle).
Class Gastropoda.
Super family Muricoidea.
Size 2³/₄in.
Locality Indo-Pacific.
Habitat depth To 83ft.

LATIRUS INFUNDIBULUM BROWN-LINED LATIRUS

This tall-spired but stocky shell is elongate
and rather slender. It has a short, open
canal, and the strong rounded axial ribs
are crossed by fine raised spiral cords
which can be brown or, as in the
depicted shell, orange on a beige or
cream background. There is a part-open
umbilicus. It dwells in offshore waters.

Family Fasciolariidae (Tulip and
Spindle).
Class Gastropoda.
Super family Muricoidea.
Size 3in.
Locality Florida, West Indies to Brazil.
Habitat depth To 83ft.

F A S C I O L A R I I D A E

LATIRUS NODATUS KNOBBED LATIRUS

A strong, rather thick shell, it has a tall spire and open canal of moderate length. The whorls bear strong low rounded axial ribs of nodules, and several raised spiral cords encircle the exterior of the canal. The shell is a dull beige color when the thick brown periostracum is removed and the aperture is a beautiful coral pink.

Family Fasciolariidae (Tulip and Spindle).
Class Gastropoda.
Super family Muricoidea.
Size 3in.
Locality Indo-Pacific.
Habitat depth To 83ft.

LIVONIA MAMMILLA MAMMAL VOLUTE

The large ovate mammal volute has a conspicuous rounded and calloused protoconch. The lip is expanded and flaring. It is generally pale orange or cream, with occasional brown tent markings on the exterior and a rich orange aperture. Endemic to South-Eastern Australia, it is dredged in deep waters.

Family Volutidae (The Volutes).
Class Gastropoda.
Super family Muricoidea.
Size 10in.
Locality South-Eastern Australia.
Habitat depth 495–1650ft.

CYMBIOLA FLAVICANS YELLOW VOLUTE

A solid, rather bulbous volute, it has a low spire. The body whorl tapers at the anterior, and the lip is flared. There are four strong columella plaits. The shell is a pale cream yellow, with hazy gray axial markings overlaid with small tan dots, and irregular lines. A shallow-water species.

Family Volutidae (The Volutes).
Class Gastropoda.
Super family Muricoidea.
Size 3in.
Locality New Guinea to Northern Australia.
Habitat depth To 83ft.

MELO AMPHORA AUSTRALIAN BALER

This largest species in the volute family— the shells were used by Aborigines and the islanders of the Torres Strait for baling out their dugouts. This is another species that Taiwanese fishermen have poached from the waters off Northern Australia, to such an extent that shells are more readily available in Taiwan than Australia.

Family Volutidae (The Volutes).
Class Gastropoda.
Super family Muricoidea.
Size 12in.
Locality Australia.
Habitat depth To 83ft.

V O L U T I D A E

AMORAI EXOPTANDA DESIRABLE VOLUTE

A heavy and solid shell, endemic to
Southern Australia, it has a large body
whorl with a high rounded shoulder, the
spire is low. There are three strong
columella pleats, and a glazed calloused
fascoile. The aperture is a beautiful,
deep orange, and the exterior markings
consist of many fine brown tent markings
and haphazard squiggles.

Family Volutidae (The Volutes).
Class Gastropoda.
Super family Muricoidea.
Size 3¹/₂ in.
Locality Southern Australia.
Habitat depth To 83ft.

  3½in

AMPULLA PRIAMUS SPOTTED FLASK

A lightweight and globose shell, the
spotted flask has an enlarged body
whorl with high rounded shoulders.
Glossy and smooth, it is a dark beige
color with rows of well-spaced small
brown squares or spots. It is a popular
collectors' shell.

Family Volutidae (The Volutes).
Class Gastropoda.
Super family Muricoidea.
Size 2¹/₄ in.
Locality North-East Atlantic.
Habitat depth To 83ft.

  2¼in

VOLUTIDAE

HARPA ARTICULARIS ARTICULATE HARP

A large, fairly lightweight shell, it has a rather inflated body whorl. The strong ribs vary in thickness from shell to shell, but have conspicuous black or gray purple broad spiral bands on them. The columella and parietal wall are glazed dark brown throughout. Both the shells depicted are from the Philippines.

Family Harpidae (Harp Shells).
Class Gastropoda.
Super family Muricoidea.
Size 3½in.
Locality Indo-Pacific.
Habitat depth To 83ft.

3½in

VASUM FLINDERSI FLINDER'S VASE

This is better known by its subgeneric name *Altivasum* and is possibly the largest of the vase shells. Shells are frequently trawled dead-collected, but live-taken specimens are scarce. Colors vary from white through to peach and deep orange.

Family Vasidae (Vase Shells).
Class Gastropoda.
Super family Muricoidea.
Size 6in.
Locality Southern and Western Australia.
Habitat depth 83–1650ft.

6in

COLUMBARIUM NATALENSE NATAL PAGODA SHELL

The smallest species of pagoda shell, it has a tall spire, long open canal, strongly corded whorls and spinose shoulders. The suture is impressed. The depicted specimen was found off Durban, where the species is endemic.

Family Vasidae (Vase Shells).
Class Gastropoda.
Super family Muricoidea.
Size 3¼in.
Locality South Africa.
Habitat depth 83–495ft.

3¼in

OLIVA INCRASSATA BURCH'S ANGLED OLIVE

A lovely color form of *O. incrassata,* this is considered by some experts to be endemic to the Gulf of California, but the two shown here are from Chile. The mottled shell is possibly a transitional form between *O. burchorum* and *O. incrassata.* This pale orange shell rarely reaches the size of its more common counterpart.

Family Olividae (Olive Shells).
Class Gastropoda.
Super family Muricoidea.
Size 2in.
Locality Chile.
Habitat depth To 83ft.

2in

OLIVIDAE / VASIDAE

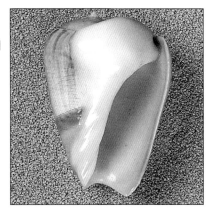

OLIVANCILLARIA URCEUS BEAR ANCILLA

A triangular shell, it has a flat heavily
calloused spire and straight-sided body
whorl. The parietal wall is thickened and
calloused, extending down to the
columella. The pale gray shells bear
numerous axial growth striae.

Family Olividae (Olive Shells).
Class Gastropoda.
Super family Muricoidea.
Size 1¼ in.
Locality Brazil and Argentina.
Habitat depth To 83ft.

MARGINELLA DESJARDINI DESJARDIN'S MARGINELLA

A beautifully marked and colored shell
margin, it is fusiform, with a long gently
tapering body whorl. The spire is low
and calloused. The depicted specimen,
which shows typical colors and pattern,
is from Senegal.

Family Olividae (Olive Shells).
Class Gastropoda.
Super family Muricoidea.
Size 2in.
Locality West Africa.
Habitat depth 83–495ft.

O

L

I

V

I

D

A

E

MITRA FRAGA STRAWBERRY MITRE

An attractive shell, with strong spiral cords, its suture is slightly impressed and the whorls have rather convex sides. The color is variable, ranging from pale orange to deep red; some examples have pale spots on the cords. The lip is finely crenellated.

Family Mitridae (Mitre Shells).
Class Gastropoda.
Super family Muricoidea.
Size 1³/₄ in.
Locality Indo-Pacific.
Habitat depth To 83ft.

1¾in

PTERYGIA FENESTRATA

A small solid mitre, it is elongated and ovate, with a low spire. The aperture is long and narrow. There are several small sharp columella folds. The shell is coarsely sculptured, its low axial ribs intersected with spiral grooves creating a nodulose texture.

Family Olividae (Olive Shells).
Class Gastropoda.
Super family Muricoidea.
Size 1³/₈ in.
Locality Indo-Pacific.
Habitat depth To 83ft.

1⅜in

CANCELLARIA SPENGLERIANA SPENGLER'S NUTMEG

A Nutmeg shell restricted in range to
Japanese waters. It is a very handsome
shell, both in proportion and
sculpturing. As can be seen from the
depicted shell, a reticulated texture
typical of Nutmegs is evident. The
axial ribbing develops into fairly sharp
nodules at the shoulders.

Family Canellariidae (Nutmeg Shells).
Class Gastropoda.
Super family Cancellarioidea.
Size 2in.
Locality Japan.
Habitat depth To 83ft.

 2in

CONUS TEXTILE TEXTILE CONE

A most common yet beautiful species,
it is popular with collectors. The textile
cone has many forms and variation,
giving rise to numerous names. The
smaller 'blue' form shown alongside
the typically marked and colored
specimen is known as *C.euetrios*.

Family Conidae (Cone Shells).
Class Gastropoda.
Super family Conoidea.
Size 3in.
Locality Indo-Pacific.
Habitat depth To 83ft.

 3in

TURRIS UNDOSA

A fusiform shell, it has a very tall, sharply tapering spire and a relatively short body whorl with a moderate open canal. There are both fine and strong rounded spiral cords. The aperture, columella and canal are pale purple. The rest of the shell is off-white, with mid-brown streaks and patches.

Family Turridae (Turrid Shells).
Class Gastropoda.
Super family Conoidea.
Size 3¼ in.
Locality Philippines.
Habitat depth 83– 495ft.

THATCHERIA MIRABILIS MIRACULOUS THATCHER SHELL

This is a wonderful pagoda-like lightweight shell of elegant proportions. A deep-water species, it is still regularly fished off Taiwan, but in recent years large and usually paler specimens have been trawled off Western Australia in water 825ft deep.

Family Turridae (Turrid Shells).
Class Gastropoda.
Super family Conoidea.
Size 3in.
Locality Japan to North-Western Australia.
Habitat depth 495–1650ft.

T U R R I D A E

APLUSTRUM AMPLUSTRE ROYAL PAPER BUBBLE

An attractive Bubble Shell, it has an ovate shape and a flat spire; the suture is channelled. The shell is patterned with two broad pink and four thin black spiral bands on a white background. This particular specimen displays a good color, though many are very dull in appearance.

Family Hydatinidae (Bubble Shells).
Class Gastropoda.
Super family Philinoidea.
Size 1in.
Locality Indo-Pacific.
Habitat depth To 83ft.

  1in

BULLA STRIATA COMMON ATLANTIC BUBBLE

This fairly sturdy bubble shell is usually ovate, with a depressed spire. The body whorl is compressed at the posterior end. Shells are most variable in pattern and color, but all have white, brown and gray hazy blotches; the aperture is white. These two specimens were collected at Yucatan, Mexico.

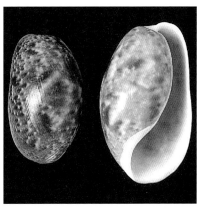

Family Hydatinidae (Bubble Shells).
Class Gastropoda.
Super family Philinoidea.
Size 1¼in.
Locality Florida to Brazil and Mediterranean.
Habitat depth To 83ft.

 1¼in

GLYCYMERIS GIGANTEA GIANT BITTERSWEET

This attractive shell has rounded, thick and very heavy symmetrical valves with low umbones and a long narrow and deep escutcheon. There is a very obvious row of coarse toxodont teeth, and the white interior has some purple or brown staining.

Family Glycimerididae (Bittersweet Clams).
Class Bivalvia.
Super family Limopsoidea.
Size 4in.
Locality Gulf of California.
Habitat depth To 83ft.

PTERIA PENGUIN PENGUIN WING OYSTER

An ovate and fairly fragile shell, it has unequal valves, the upper, or right, valve being more inflated. The depicted specimen clearly shows the characteristic extension of the hinge line. As in the case with most oysters, parts of the shell expand and crack when they are in a dry warm atmosphere.

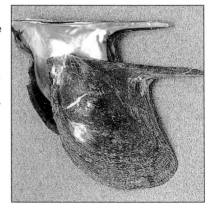

Family Pteriidae (Wing and Pearl Oysters).
Class Bivalvia.
Super family Pterioidea.
Size 6in.
Locality Indo-Pacific.
Habitat depth To 83ft.

OSTREA EDULIS COMMON EUROPEAN OYSTER

This is the edible oyster of the gourmet and farmed on a commercial basis. It is roughly circular, the upper valve being inflated, the lower virtually flat. The interior is greyish white and smooth; the exterior is covered with rugged layers of radial ribs and scales and is beige or gray in color.

Family Ostreidae (True Oysters).
Class Bivalvia.
Super family Ostreoidea.
Size 3in.
Locality Western Europe and Mediterranean.
Habitat depth To 83ft.

ARGOPECTEN PURPURATUS PURPLE SCALLOP

Another commercially fished edible species, this is a large shell, its valves being equal, and rounded and less inflated than those of other *Argopecten* species. The strong and fat radial ribs are a deep purple on a white background, the colors being more vivid on the upper valve. The interior pallial line is tinged with purple.

Family Pectinidae (Scallop Shells).
Class Bivalvia.
Super family Pectinoidea.
Size 4in.
Locality Western South America.
Habitat depth To 83ft.

ACANTHOCARDIA TUBERCULATA TUBERCULATE COCKLE

A solid species, the Tuberculate Cockle has equal and inflated valves and very large rounded umbones, which in some shells touch and erode each other. There are prominent, rounded radial ribs. The color can be attractive, cream or beige and with a pale orange to brown tint on the interior.

Family Cardiidae (Cockle Shells).
Class Bivalvia.
Super family Cardioidea.
Size 2¹/₂ in.
Locality Southern England to Mediterranean, Canary Islands.
Habitat depth To 495ft.

  2½in

PLAGIOCARDIUM PSEUDOLIMA GIANT HEART COCKLE

This is one of the largest of the cockles, with rounded-to-ovate very inflated and heavy valves. The numerous low radial ribs bear small thick scaly spines. The depicted specimen, which comes from Mombasa, shows typical color, but albino shells occasionally occur.

Family Cardiidae (Cockle Shells).
Class Bivalvia.
Super family Cardioidea.
Size 6in.
Locality East Africa.
Habitat depth To 83ft.

  8in

TRIDACNA GIGAS GIANT CLAM

This is the largest and heaviest known mollusc—the two valves can weigh as much as 500lb. The elongated-oval shell, with its equal valves, has about five very large undulating and rounded ribs, with numerous concentric growth striae. Mature shells are encrusted with lime deposits and much marine debris.

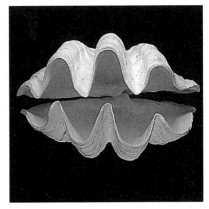

Family Tridacnidae (Giant Clams).
Class Bivalvia.
Super family Tridacnoidea.
Size 3ft.
Locality South-West Pacific.
Habitat depth To 83ft.

LIOCONCHA CASTRENSIS CHOCOLATE-FLAMED VENUS

This is a most attractive Venus Clam. The rounded-to-oval shell has equal and somewhat inflated valves with fine concentric ridges. It is cream in color, with hazy grayish blue patches, overlaid with vivid dark brown zigzag lines or tent markings.

Family Veneridae (Venus Clams).
Class Bivalvia.
Super family Veneroidea.
Size 2in.
Locality Indo-Pacific.
Habitat depth To 83ft.

NAUTILUS POMPILIUS COMMON CHAMBERED NAUTILUS

This species has a large coiled shell, with an indented spire and gaping aperture. The shell is off-white, with distinctive tan, radial bands. There is a black calloused area facing the aperture. The half-section shows the internal chambers which are used as a buoyancy aid.

Family Nautilidae (Chambered Nautilus Shells).
Class Cephalopoda.
Super family None.
Size 15cm (6in).
Locality Western Pacific.
Habitat depth 25–500m (83–495ft).

ARGONAUTA ARGO COMMON PAPER NAUTLUS

This beautiful delicate structure is very thin and lightweight. There are numerous low wavy radial ridges, where a double row of short sharp nodules extends around the shell. The shell is off-white to cream in color, the early part of the keel and spines being tinted with grayish black.

Family Argonautidae (Paper Nautilus).
Class Cephalopoda.
Super family Argonautoidea.
Size 8in.
Locality Worldwide in warm seas.
Habitat depth To 83ft.

Index
Alphabetical listing of scientific names.

I N D E X

Index Alphabetical listing of common names.